Fun With Hieroglyphs: Easy Egyptian Fun

Speedy Publishing LLC
40 E. Main St. #1156
Newark, DE 19711

www.speedypublishing.com

Copyright 2015
9781681453767
First Printed February 3, 2015

SPHINXES
AFRICA
EGYPT
BEDOUIN
GIZA
PYRAMID
PHARAOH
OSIRIS

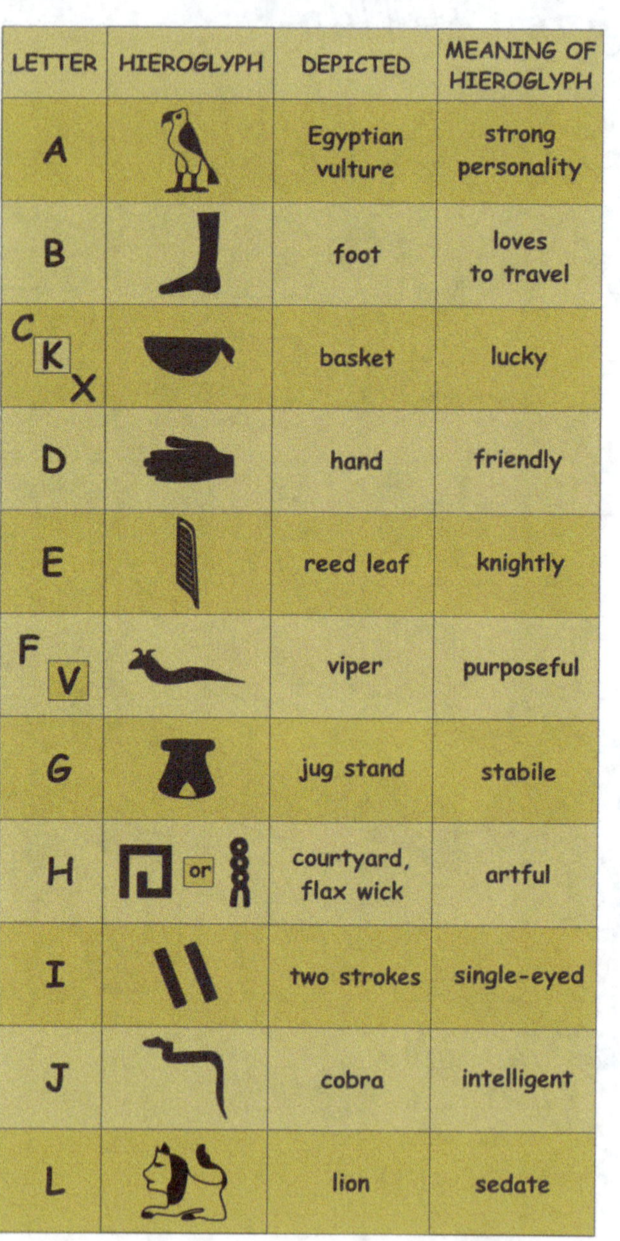

LETTER	HIEROGLYPH	DEPICTED	MEANING OF HIEROGLYPH
A		Egyptian vulture	strong personality
B		foot	loves to travel
C / K		basket	lucky
D		hand	friendly
E		reed leaf	knightly
F / V		viper	purposeful
G		jug stand	stabile
H		courtyard, flax wick	artful
I		two strokes	single-eyed
J		cobra	intelligent
L		lion	sedate

MEANING OF HIEROGLYPH	DEPICTED	HIEROGLYPH	LETTER
wise	owl		M
pure soul	Red Crown, water surface		N
optimist	lasso		O
able to create	wicker seat		P
—	hillside		Q
talkative	mouth		R
independent	folded cloth, bolt		S
loves to eat	bread		T
obstinate	quail chick		U / W
equitable	two reed leaf		Y
capricious	bolt		Z

A

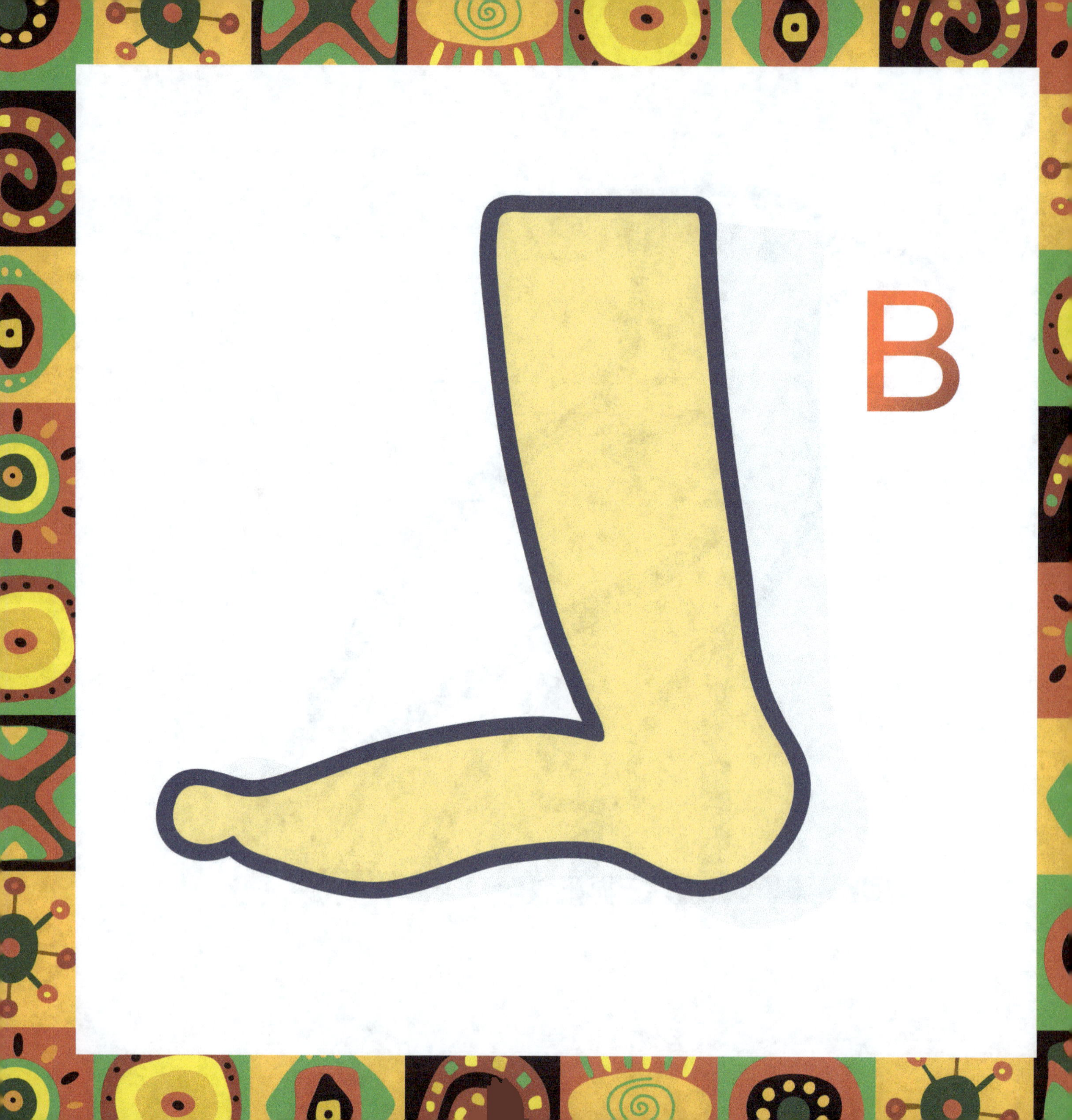
B

C

D

E

F

G

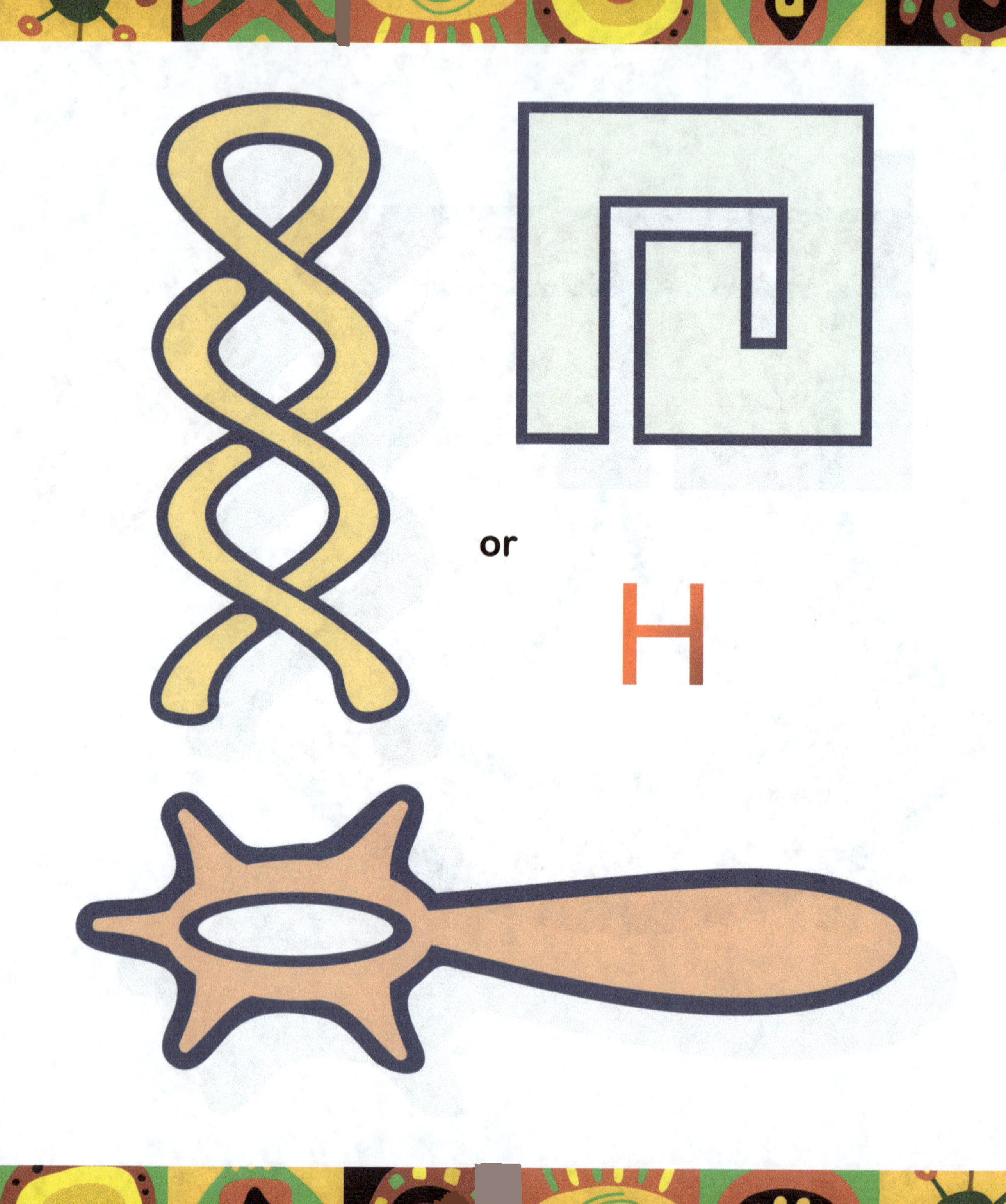
or
H

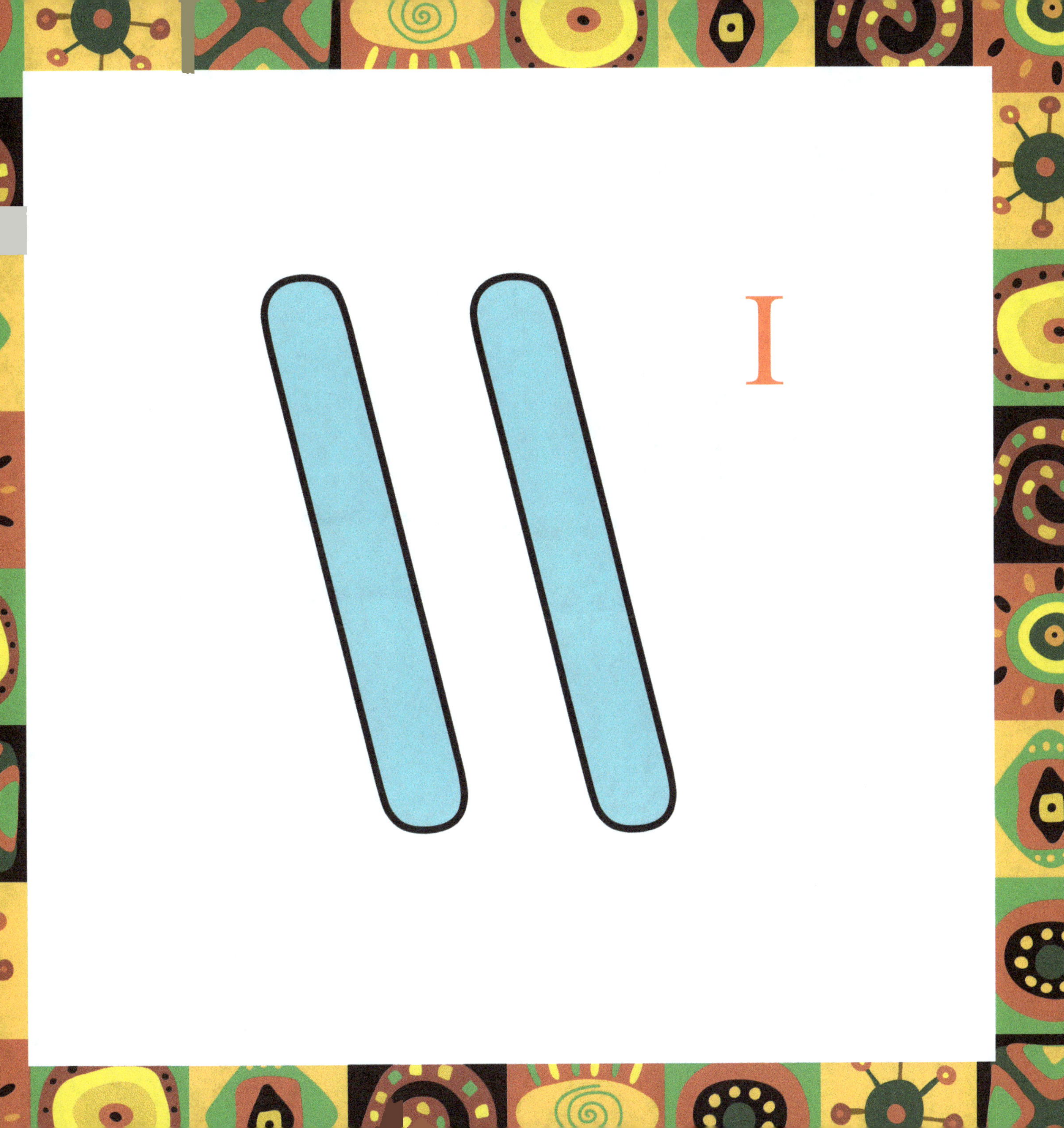
I

J

K

L

M

N

P

Q

R

s

T

U
W

U

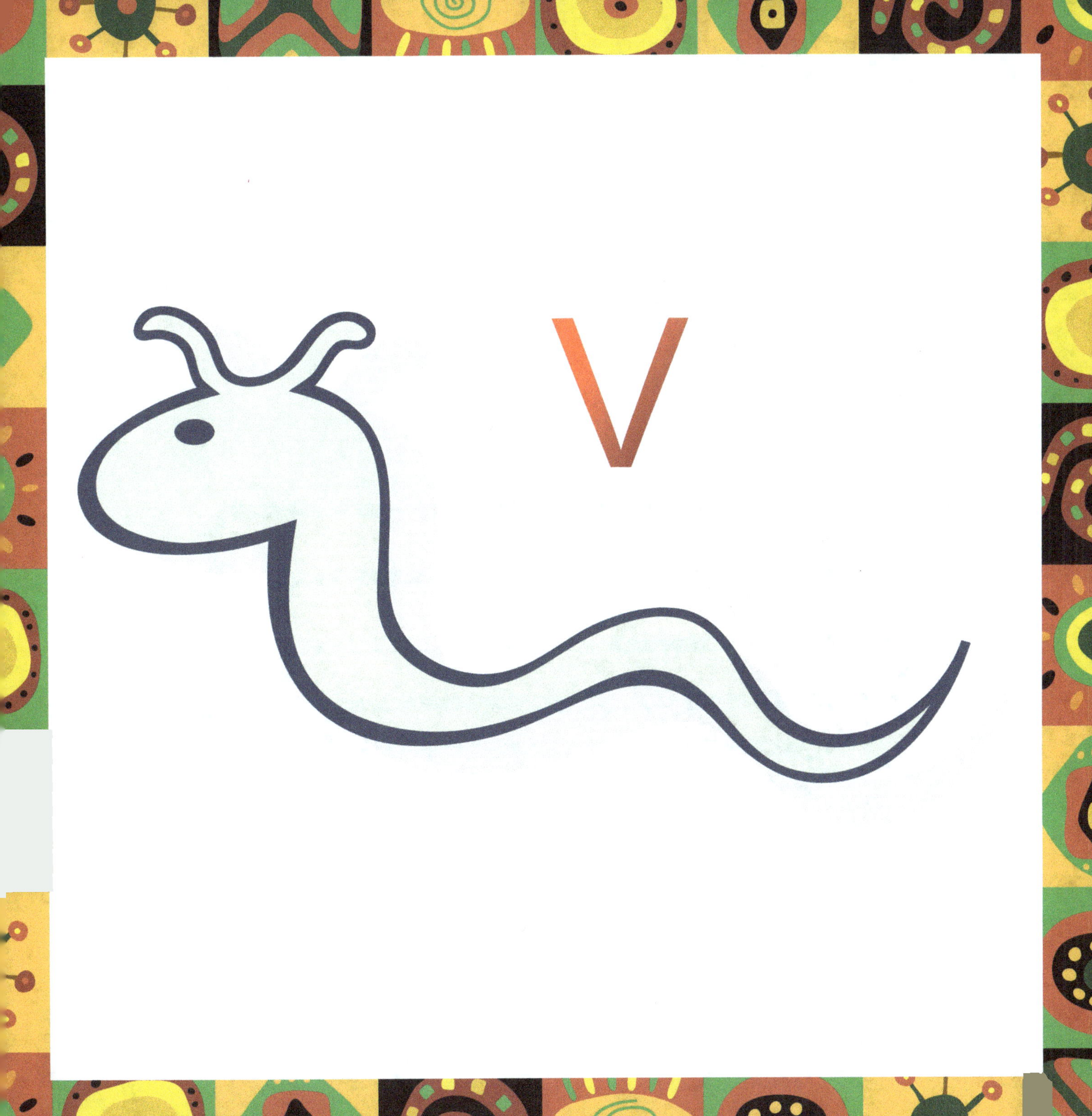

v

X

Y

z

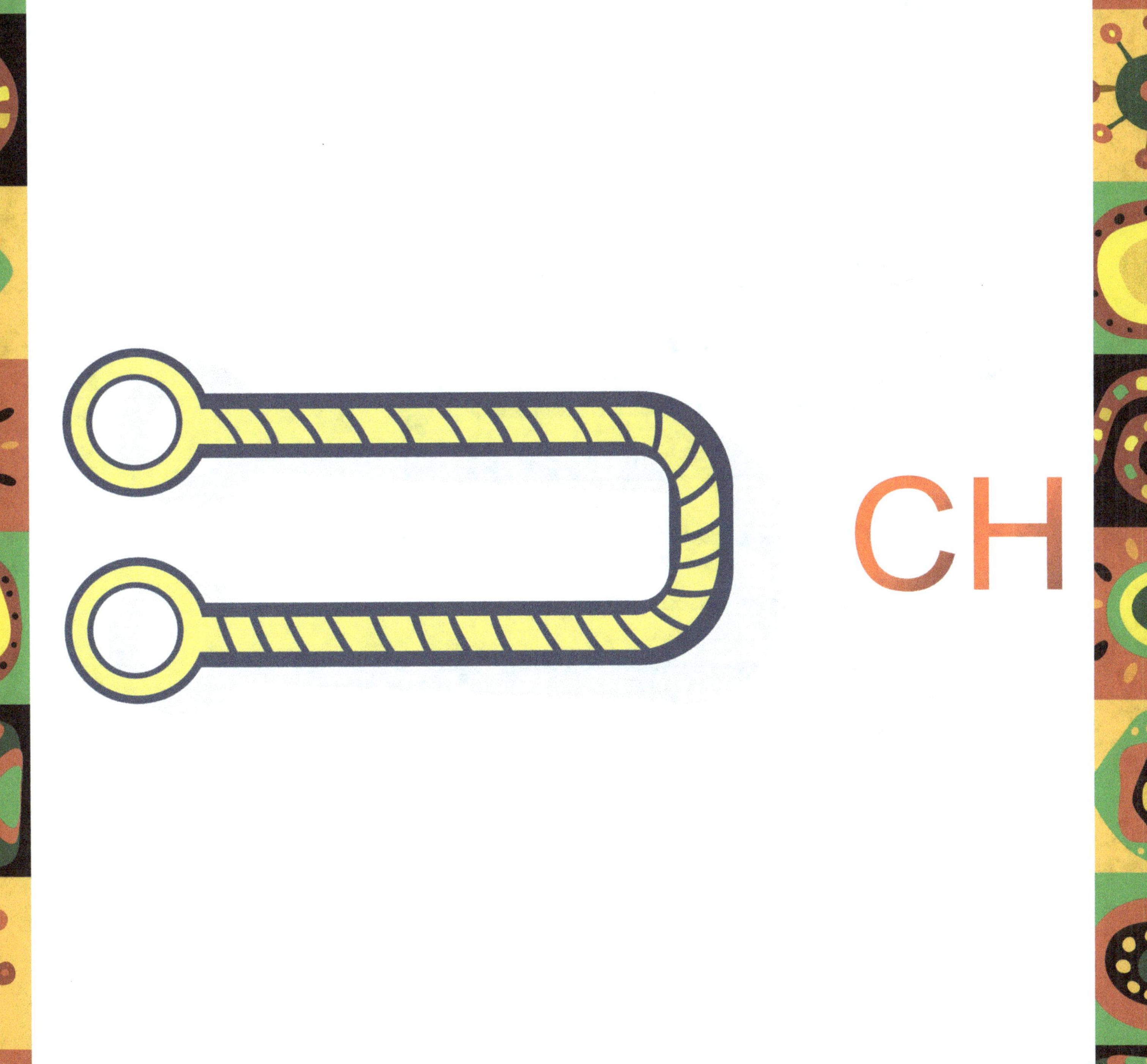
CH

KH

Egyptian Gods and Goddesses

Ra
'Sun'
God of sun.

Geb and Nut

Geb is the God of the earth and Nut is the Goddess of the sky.

Isis
Goddess of magic.

Seth
God of
chaos.

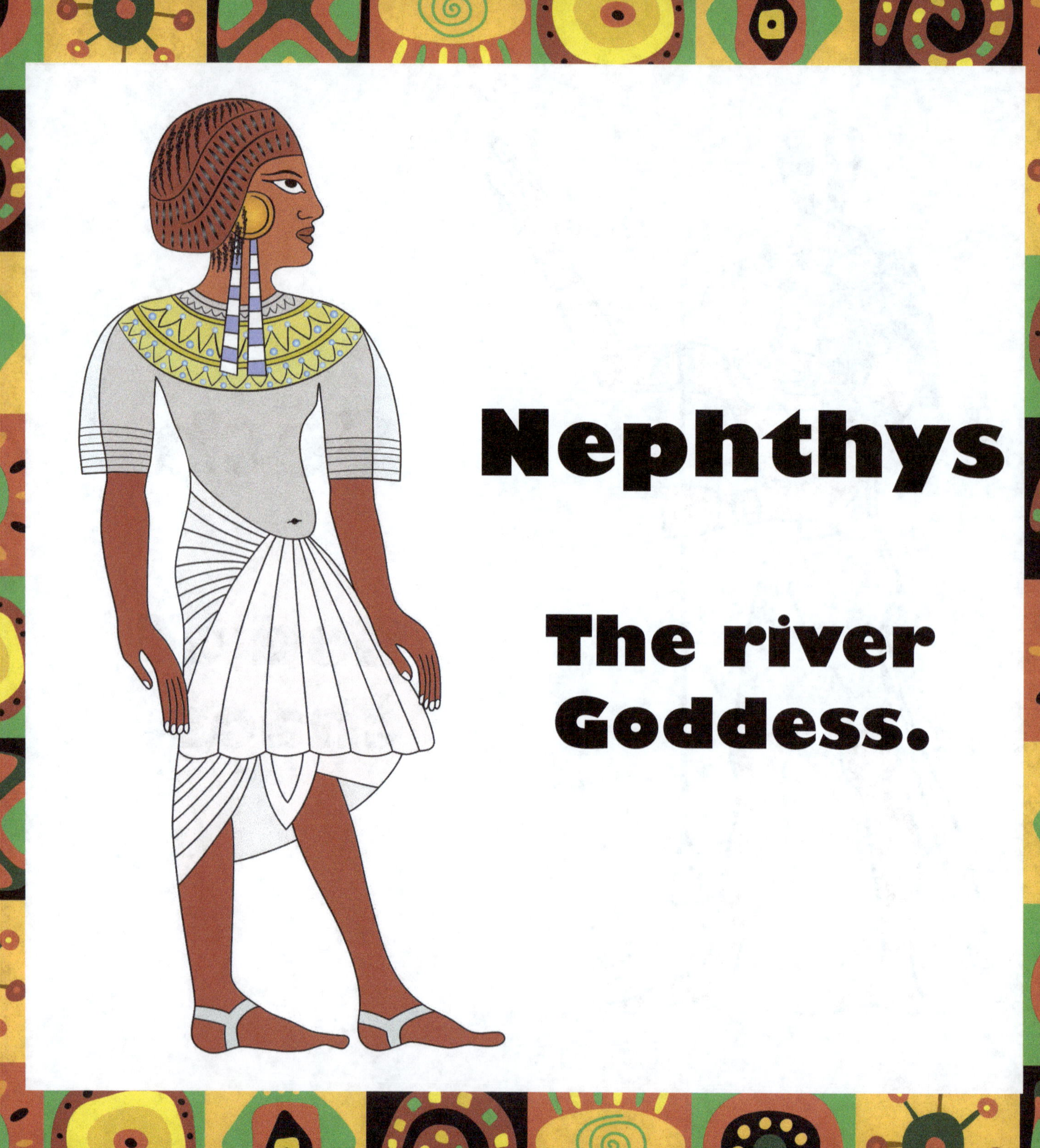

Nephthys

The river
Goddess.

Horus
God of the sky.

Anubis

God of embalming and the dead.

Hathor

Goddess of love and joy.

Khnum
God of the
innundation.

Ma'at

**Goddess
of truth,
justice and
harmony.**

Sekhmet
Goddess of war.

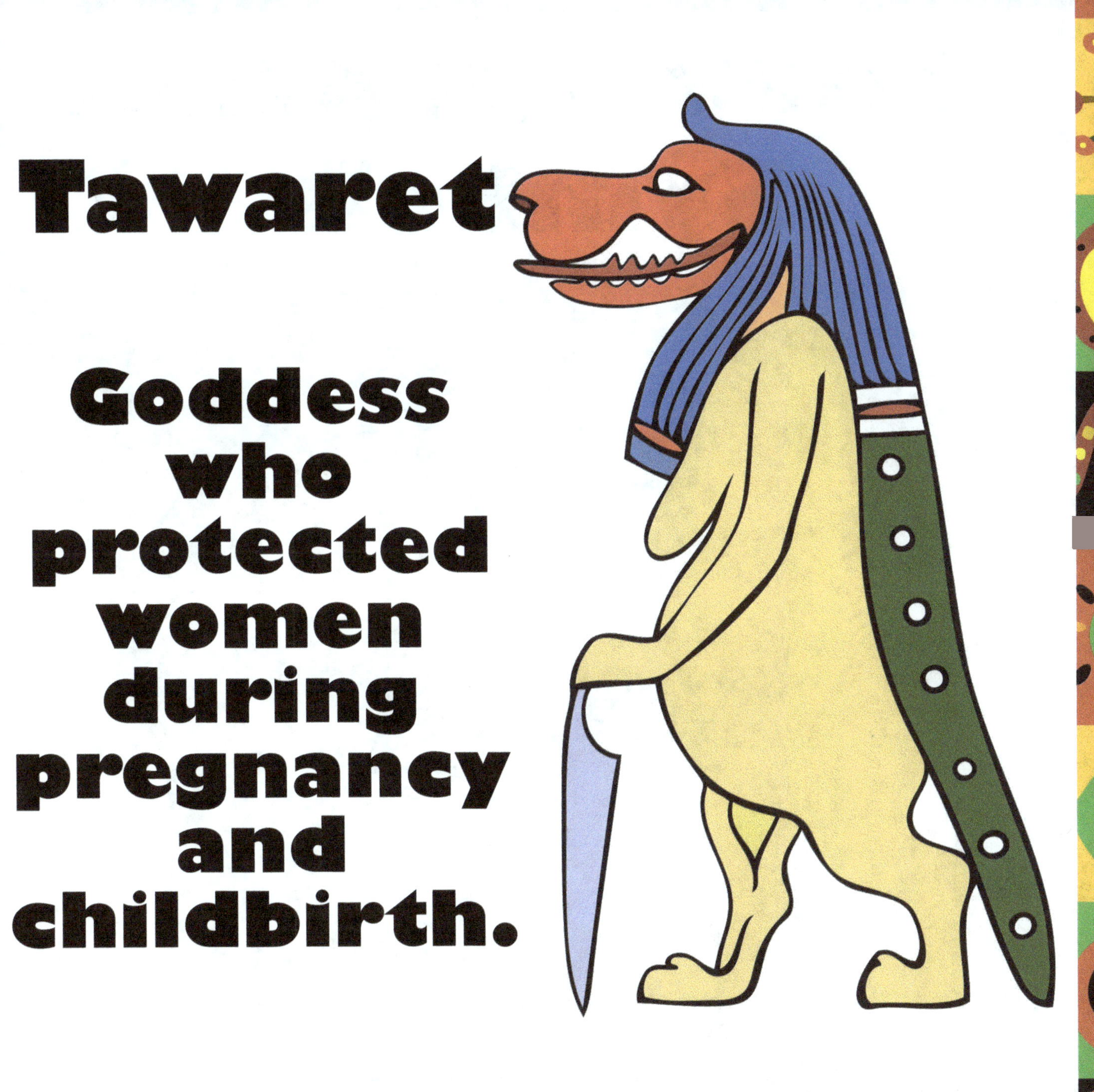

Tawaret

Goddess
who
protected
women
during
pregnancy
and
childbirth.

Other Egyptian Symbols

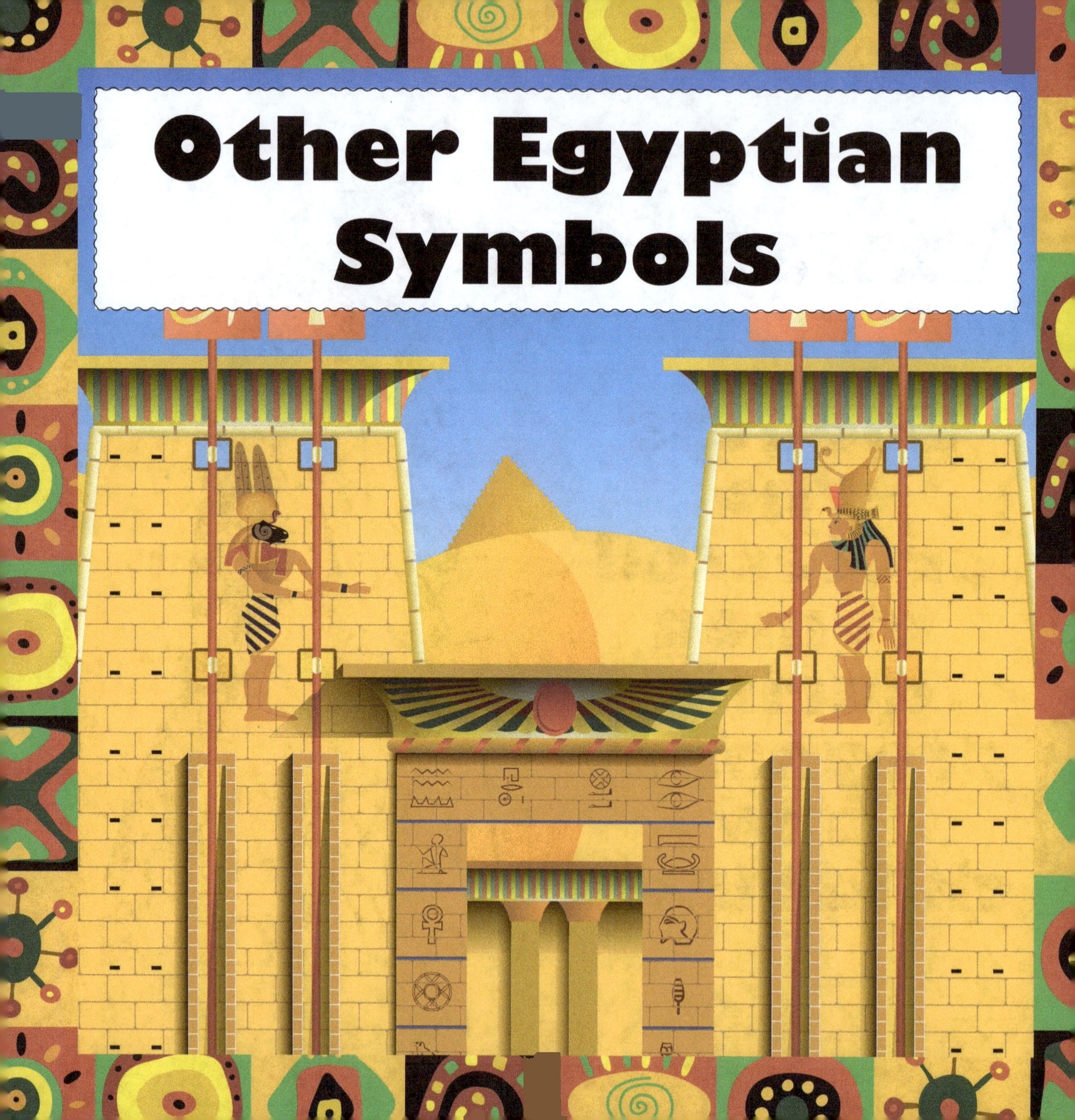

Astrological Symbols

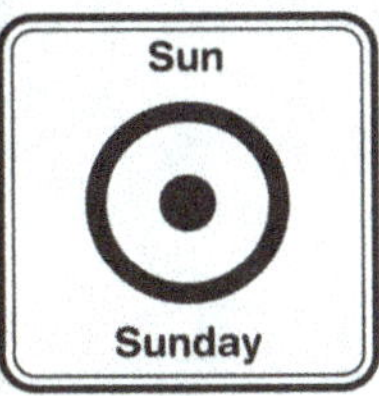
Sun / Sunday

New Moon / Monday

Moon / 1st Quarter

Moon / Last Quarter

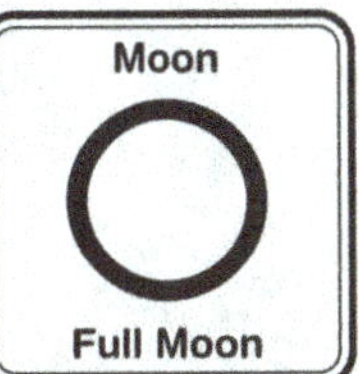
Moon / Full Moon

Earth / Global Cluster

Mars / Tuesday

Mercury / Wednesday

Jupiter / Thursday

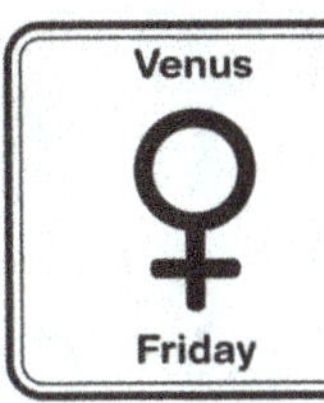
Venus / Friday

Saturn / Saturday

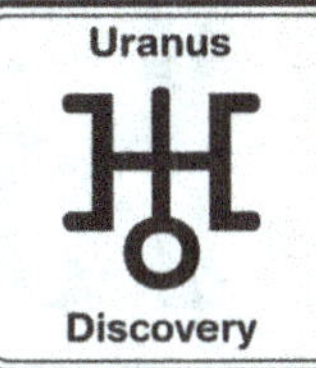
Uranus / Discovery

Pluto / Monogram PL

Neptune / Trident

Earth / Globe & Cross

Uranus / Mistery

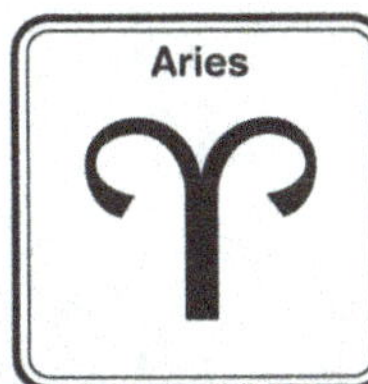
Aries

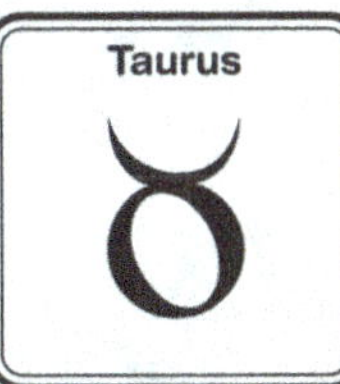
Taurus

Gemini

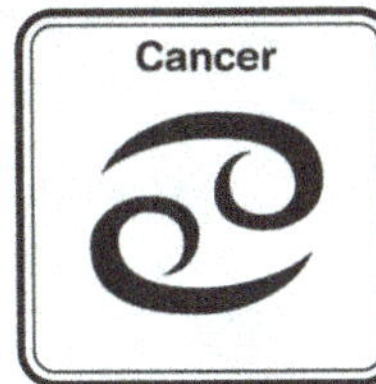
Cancer

Leo

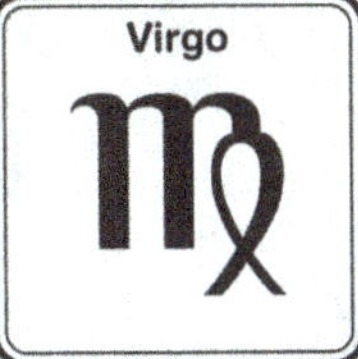
Virgo

Libra

Scorpio

Sagitarius

Capricorn

Aquarius

Pisces